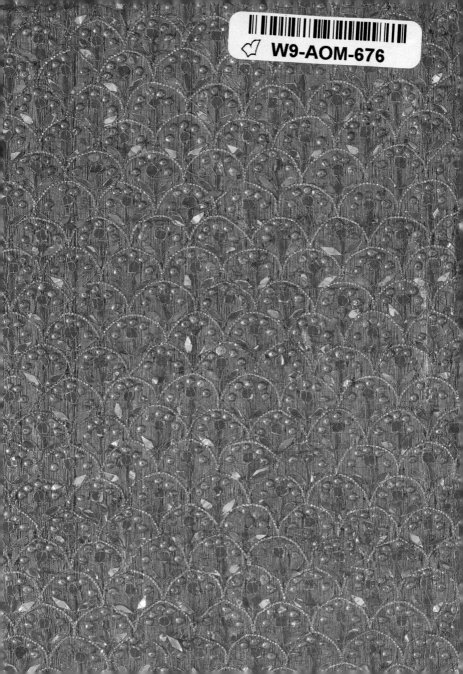

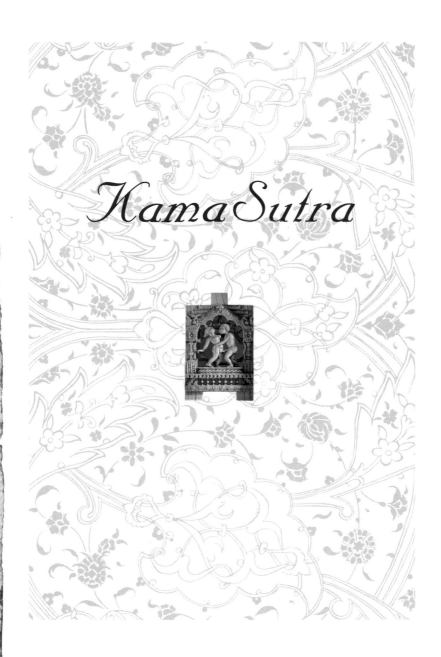

KamaSutra

This edition published by Barnes & Noble, Inc., by
arrangement with The Book Laboratory™ Inc.

2003 Barnes & Noble Books

Printed in Malaysia

Library of Congress Cataloging-in-Publication Data is available
upon request.

ISBN 0-7607-4289-8

M 10 9 8 7 6 5 4 3 2 1

First Edition

Contents

O Gautam! Woman is sacrificial fire, agni;
her mons veneris is sacrificial altar, vedi;
addressing and chanting is its burning, genitalia is flame,
and penetration is fire;
the consequential bliss is its sparking.
When the gods dedicate their semen into the sacrificial fire
that is woman the result is procreation.
—CHANDOGYA UPANISHAD V:8.1-2

All the great religious traditions of the world revere sacred scriptures. These include the Buddhist Dhammapada, the Islamic Qur'an, the Christian New Testament, the Judaic Torah, the Confucian Analects, the Vedas and the Bhagavad Gita of the Hindus, and many more. Sacred scriptures contain essential spiritual truths. They are of immense historical value because they have influenced the minds, hearts, and behavior of billions of people from the ancient past until today. Sacred scriptures in all wisdom traditions deal with morality, the right path, faith, belief, enlightenment, and, ultimately with the eternal life of the spirit and its link to the divine.

Within Hinduism we find the most rare of sacred scriptures, the Kama Sutra, an ancient text that teaches us how to make love well and joyously. In its introduction, the text declares that knowing how to make love is as essential to the training of the spirit as meditation and spiritual practice. The Kama Sutra intimates in this unusual proposition that our

body is a temple and that to know the nature of desire is the first step in the long quest of knowing oneself. The Kama Sutra gives the practitioner the power to channel sexuality in such a way that it becomes a source of deep experience, self-knowledge, and fulfillment. In this practice, the body becomes the training ground for deep meditation. The Kama Sutra is a manual set out in sutras, or teachings, that informs and trains us to be not only skilled lovers but deeply knowledgeable about love practices, from sexual positions to understanding how men and women behave together intimately.

Many spiritual traditions tragically deny the pleasures of the body for the sake of pursuing the divine. There has rarely been joyous complicity between body and spirit; in fact, religion has almost single-handedly fueled division and conflict between the two. The Kama Sutra is like a drop of nectar in the bareness of this ground of being: It fertilizes the mind and the spirit and invites us to heal the bitter divide between sexuality and spirituality. A truly religious person seeks non-duality: To accept the beauty of sexuality is thus the first step toward a true understanding of religiousness. To love—physically as well as in every other way—is a sacred mystery.

The Kama Sutra is also a tribute to a millennia old culture that honored and valued sexuality as part of sacred life. These texts provide us with a fascinating portrait of ancient India, whose openness to sexuality gave rise to a highly sophisticated practice of the erotic.

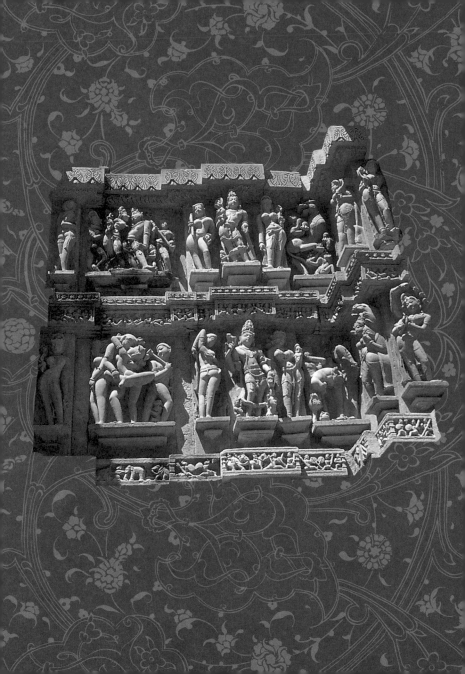

About the Frieze

The statue you find in this box is a replica of a frieze from the walls of one of the temples in the Khajuraho complex in central India. The Chandella kings, who rose to power between 950 and 1050 C.E., built this temple city in a valley surrounded on all sides by hills. The temples survived the later Mughal rule of India, which, so piously Muslim in character, would have destroyed them had its rulers known of the existence of the complex. Thick jungles and difficult terrain sheltered the temples, and so they remained in obscurity until recently, when the Indian government restored them and opened them to the public in 1999. The Khajuraho complex was built as a symbol of *bhakti*, or Indian devotional worship. Beautiful bas-reliefs of men and women making love were carved on pillars, brackets, lintels, and niches from top to bottom. The figures are positioned in every way possible for two bodies to conjoin, and include scenes of group sex. Far from inelegant, the Khajuraho figures assume dance and yogic postures, and with their graceful limbs and forms evince a mysterious erotic interplay of deep shadows and bewitching shapes.

The temples celebrate the union of Shiva and Shakti. Shiva is one of the greatest of all Hindu gods. With Brahma and Vishnu, he forms a tri-umvirate, the trimurti, a single body divided in three godly shapes. Shakti, whose name means "power," is his consort. Through her, Shiva manifests his power of creation and destruction. The sexual act is thus seen as the eternal beginning and ending of the power of life, always being born and always dying. The Khajuraho figures, immortalized for centuries in friezes such as the one with this book, are reminders of the sacred dimension of sexuality. When we make love we can attain a state of sensory perception that opens us to greater dimensions of experience.

This gift box you hold in your hands is a reminder for you of your own highest wisdom and your innate power to experience the divine when you make love. Place the Khajuraho frieze on the nightstand by your bed, on your home altar, in a place of power, or wherever it looks beautiful; every time you look at the frieze, allow it to remind you of the unfolding of your spiritual power, of the power of change in your life, and of new beginnings waiting to happen. Ideally, the Khajuraho lovers should sit peacefully in an empty space, so that their presence can create a field of energy—a space for you to change, an atmosphere of serenity and of trust that will help show you that the highest aspirations are indeed attainable. Divine love enfolds all things and all beings completely, and its presence in your life will introduce a new dimension of being and of loving.

May the power of divine love be with you and guide you in your relationships, and help you transform every sexual act into a prayer of devotion and gratitude.

—MANUELA DUNN MASCETTI, JANUARY 2000

The Kama Sutra

An ancient Indian legend tells that the first rules of love, known as *kama shastra* in Sanskrit, were given to mankind by the white bull Nandin, Shiva's faithful companion. They were Shiva's gift to men and women to remind them of his power of creation every time they made love. An interest in the sensual perception of life has always pervaded Indian myth and thought, and several authors wrote treatises on the erotic sciences as early as the eighth century B.C.E. Vatsyayana, a Brahman Sanskrit scholar who lived in a city called Pataliputra (today called Patna) in the fourth century B.C.E., became known as the ultimate compiler of the rules of erotic love and practice. In order to make the material more accessible to readers, Vatsyayana collected all the previous writings of the *kama shastra* and reorganized them into the Kama Sutra, which soon became the classical treatise on the subject.

The word *kama* means "erotic practice" in Sanskrit. Eroticism is the search for pleasure, and the goal of these teachings is to attain the perception of the divine state that is infinite delight. The Kama Sutra thus became an ancillary text to the sacred works of Hinduism. Adepts were encouraged to practice the art of lovemaking as one would practice any other physical and spiritual discipline—by deepening their understanding of the erotic and by approaching sexuality as sacred. The Kama Sutra is thus not a sex manual, nor is it pornographic; on the contrary, when we read it we are surprised by its natural and sensitive character, and we become enchanted by its guidelines on the varied and infinite ways of loving another. In ancient India, elegant men and women were encouraged to study the Kama Sutra as they should study treatises of the arts and sciences.

As in many Hindu technical works, the text of the Kama Sutra is written in condensed, versified form—sutras—meant to be memorized. Commentaries on the sutras accompany the verses, and are integral parts of the teaching. The sutras address the whole spectrum of the game of love and seduction, including homosexual practices, inversion of roles, marriage, infidelity, prostitution, and love and healing potions. In this book we explore the first two sections of the Kama Sutra: the foundation of love and the techniques of lovemaking and a further section on the subject of infidelity. The original text contains many more sections, called in their totality "The Sixty-Four Arts."

Paradoxically, the tone of the Kama Sutra is dispassionate, describing positions in a technical way, following schemes and including rules of what should and should not be practiced. This perhaps proves how much it has been used as an educative manual—almost a social science—as if the poetry of love were taken for granted. It is not that sexuality in India was devoid of feeling, but rather that its sacred dimension was once so deeply understood that it formed a primary aspect. The finesse of the lovers on the Khajuraho temples shows that they combined sexuality with divinity, infusing everything with beauty. Exposed to the bright heat of the Indian sun, the temple figures seem to come alive with radiance in a celebration of passion in stone and light.

India in the fourth century B.C.E., the time when Vatsyayana composed the Kama Sutra, was sexually freer than it became in later centuries of Muslim invasion and Victorian British rule. The text suggests and even encourages infidelity and deceiving one's spouse. The remarriage of widows, which was later forbidden, was then accepted. And *suttee*, the burning of the wife on the husband's funereal pyre, was never mentioned in the original commentary. Homosexuality and lesbianism were accepted as part of normal sexual relations. Courtesans played a valued role in society; they performed music and dance in religious temples and served as the keepers of sacred arts. The Puritanism of later India took an oblique view of its erotic heritage and tried to dismiss it as the negative influence of Western civilization. The fact is that texts such as the Kama Sutra and erotic temples like Khajuraho predated the puritanical values that later seized the country and are only now being dispelled. Paintings of inter-course have always been part of popular Indian art, and are still seen today on pottery used in weddings because the images are considered to be good omens of fertility. Sexuality was not repressed, but accepted as a divine gift to mankind.

The erotic postures of the Kama Sutra are like the asanas in yoga, which enhance inner feelings and awaken energies that otherwise lie dormant. In the same way that yogis and yoginis learn the deeply healing silence of the body in each asana, lovers learn the ecstasy of union in each sexual posture. The approach is the same in both practices: We learn through meditation, by becoming aware.

The Foundation of Love

The full life span of a man is one hundred years.
He should pursue the three objects of Dharma, Artha, *and* Kama
at different periods in such a way that they harmonize with one another
and do not clash in any way. During childhood, he should acquire learning;
during youth and middle age he should enjoy Kama; and during old age he
should attend to Dharma in order to obtain Moksha, or final liberation.
—1.2 ON THE ATTAINMENTS OF DHARMA, ARTHA, AND KAMA

Hinduism has devised a life order by which every Hindu can attain liberation from the law of karma and rebirth: The first part of life is to be lived within society to enjoy its pleasures, and the second part is to be lived in seclusion and meditation. The first part of life is seen as training for the second half, as if each individual is a holy person in preparation. The more spiritually one lives, the greater the rewards in the second part of life. *Artha* and *Kama* are the goals of middle life: Artha is the art of acquiring possessions and wealth according to spiritual principles, and Kama is erotic practice. The harmonious practice of Artha and Kama bring fulfillment to the individual, who, having fully enjoyed the pleasures of midlife, can enter the sacredness of the later years without regrets. There is an order to life that suits the mood and temperament of each stage: If we embrace ascetic spirituality without having first fully explored sexuality, it will always unconsciously haunt our practice. But, if we come to it after having known every aspect of *samsara*—the whole cycle of life, death, and rebirth—we will experience a deeper silence and sacredness.

Thus a man who pursues the objects of Dharma, Artha,
and Kama enjoys happiness both in this world and in the next.
The wise one pursues pleasures in such a way that neither
Dharma is violated, nor the holy life is spoilt, nor Artha neglected.
—I . 2 ON THE ATTAINMENTS OF DHARMA, ARTHA, AND KAMA

Man should study the arts and sciences of the Kama Sutra along
with the studies of Dharma and Artha. Not only men, but also young girls
should study the Kama Sutra before and after marriage.
—I . 3 THE STUDY OF THE ARTS

In the above passage, Vatsyayana is pointing to classical Indian education, in which the body as well as the mind and the spirit are trained. Classical Western education also includes physical training, but the understanding of sexuality has been left off the curriculum for centuries. In India, all concerns of life are addressed, and the pupil receives a highly sophisticated training that covers ethics, economy, sciences, the arts, and erotic practices. One's understanding of the music for instance—its philosophy, moods and evocations—goes hand in hand with one's understanding of lovemaking. When man and woman are united in their sexual relationship they develop the strength and maturity to enjoy material wealth and spiritual progress in their later years. The study of the Kama Sutra thus strengthens the individual and prepares him or her for life.

THE SIXTY-FOUR FEMININE ARTS

Women in particular are encouraged to study the Kama Sutra from a young age along with the sixty-four arts that accompany and enhance erotic technique. Vatsyayana suggests that older women, perhaps mothers or aunts, should teach young girls, establishing with them a relationship of trust and instructing them in the ways of seduction and sexuality.

The sixty-four arts that enhance the teachings of the Kama Sutra:

1. *Vocal music*
2. *Instrumental music*
3. *Dance*
4. *Painting*
5. *Cutting and stenciling, especially the tilaka, the mark adorning the forehead*
6. *Decoration of the floor with colored rice grains and flowers*
7. *Flower arrangements*
8. *Henna colorings for the hands and body*
9. *Mosaics*
10. *Arranging the bed beautifully*
11. *Playing instruments made of bowls filled with water*
12. *Water games*
13. *The use of charms, drugs, and magic words*
14. *Making garlands*
15. *Making crowns and head ornaments*
16. *The art of dressing*
17. *Making and shaping ornaments made of ivory or shell*
18. *Preparing perfumes*
19. *Jewelry*
20. *Magic and the creation of illusions*
21. *Preparing lotions and ointments*
22. *Manicure*
23. *Cooking*
24. *Preparing drinks*
25. *Tailoring and needlework*
26. *Lacemaking*
27. *The art of playing the veena (a string instrument) and the damaru (a drum)*
28. *Making and solving puzzles*
29. *Reciting verse*

30. *Riddles*
31. *Quoting from books*
32. *Knowledge of dramas and short narratives*
33. *The art of completing poetic stanzas when part of them is given*
34. *Making articles from cane and bamboo*
35. *Designing ornaments in gold and silver*
36. *Carpentry*
37. *Architecture and furnishing the home*
38. *Knowledge of gems and stones*
39. *Knowledge of metals*
40. *Valuing the shape and color of stones*
41. *Gardening and treating the diseases of plants and trees*
42. *Breeding stock*
43. *Teaching parrots and mynah birds to sing*
44. *Massage and care of body and hair*
45. *Writing and understanding the symbolic gestures of theater*
46. *Knowledge of foreign languages*
47. *Knowledge of dialects and regional languages*
48. *Decorating chariots and cars with flowers*
49. *Reading omens and making spells*
50. *Understanding the workings of machinery used every day*
51. *Developing memory*
52. *Reciting verse*
53. *Composing verse*
54. *Knowledge of words and etymology*
55. *Knowledge of poetic meter*
56. *Knowledge of literary forms*
57. *The art of impersonation*
58. *The art of wearing clothes so as to conceal the body's defects*
59. *The art of gambling*
60. *Knowledge of dice games*
61. *Children's games*

62. *Good manners*
63. *Knowledge of the art of war for success*
64. *Physical exercise*
—1.3 THE STUDY OF THE ARTS

The sixty-four arts are the expressions of elegant femininity. A woman seduces not only by erotic play but also by creating a beautiful atmosphere in the home; by amusing her man with her knowledge of music, poetry, literature, theater, flower arrangements, and cooking; and even her skill in taking care of children. According to the Kama Sutra, woman is the embodiment of grace. The text encourages women to cultivate elegance and style in every aspect of life. A well-bred woman nourishes her relationships and entertains her lovers better and longer than the woman whose knowledge is only employed for sexual seduction. Good conversation, dressing well, playfulness, and intelligence are great assets in the game of love.

THE WELL-BRED CITIZEN

Having acquired learning, the well-bred citizen begins his life
with wealth acquired through inheritance, and or by business, investments,
or gifts received, and settles down to live a refined life. He should reside
in a city or town, and live close to others of his own status. He may also
for a time go traveling. His residence should be near water and should
be divided into two parts—the home and the garden.
—1.4 THE DAILY LIFE OF A WELL-BRED CITIZEN

The Kama Sutra also instructs men on how to cultivate a refined lifestyle—from keeping a home and tending a beautiful garden to balancing work and privacy. A man who works all hours is too exhausted to play the game of love. But if he learns to work and also give himself time for such pastimes such as music, friendship, theater, and the arts, he will be better disposed

to love, which requires time and attention. The perfect home for the well-bred citizen:

> *The home should have a bedroom with a beautiful bed,*
> *soft and comfortable, with many pillows on it,*
> *covered with beautiful sheets and a canopy for privacy.*
> *Next to the bed should be another bed, or perhaps a sofa,*
> *for the preliminary games of love. A low table should sit next to*
> *the second bed, for incense sticks, flowers, garlands, and perfumed oils.*
> *Close to it there should be musical instruments such as the veena,*
> *and on the floor, painting materials, ornament boxes, books, and flowers.*
> *Outside the room should be cages with parrots,, quails, and*
> *singing mynah birds. A separate room in the house should be kept*
> *for carpentry, carving, and other manual hobbies.*
> *The garden should be well kept with bowers of flowering creepers,*
> *fountains, swings, and seats for lying and sitting.*
> —1.4 THE DAILY LIFE OF THE WELL-BRED CITIZEN

According to the sutras, the home of the ideal Kama Sutra man is theatrical —a place where pleasures are pursued, a stage for entertaining friends and lovers with music, conversation, even painting and carpentry. Fragrant with constantly burning incense, this home is well lived, a place of soulfulness where the man retires after work and spends hours reading or making music. The opposite of a bachelor's pad, it is well kept and elegant, with a four-poster bed piled high with pillows, and with a garden resonant with the songs of birds and the trickle of fountains. The place of seduction is as important as one's skill at seduction, and women are always curious to find a reflection of a man's character in his surroundings. A man who has an interesting home is more interesting. His ideal day:

The well-bred citizen, having risen early in the morning,
should clean his teeth, apply moisturizers and ointments to his skin,
perform worship, decorate himself with garlands of flowers,
chew betel leaf, and then go about his daily business.
He must bathe daily, massage his body with oil every other day,
shave his beard frequently, and always disguise the smell of his sweat.
Meals should be taken twice daily, before noon and in the evening
before nightfall. After the midday meal, he should spend time quietly,
perhaps teaching parrots and mynah birds to speak or watching partridges,
cocks, or rams fighting. He may choose to inform himself of the affairs
of the day by speaking with his managers, friends, and secretaries
before resting in the afternoon. Later in the afternoon, he should indulge
in conversation with his friends. In the evening there should be music lessons.
He then returns with his friends to his home, where they wait for the arrival
of the ladies invited for the night. Either he sends a messenger to call them
or he goes to fetch them himself. After their arrival, he and his friends should
welcome them, and entertain them with loving and affectionate conversation.
Should the ladies be drenched in rain, he should change their clothes and
provide them with comfortable robes. Thus ends the well-bred citizen's day.

—1.4 THE DAILY LIFE OF THE WELL-BRED CITIZEN

The rhythm of India is slow and leisurely, and so the well-bred citizen has time for both work and enjoyment. Even if the rules of the Kama Sutra don't fit into the Western pace of life, they point at something that is sorely lacking in most men's lives: entertainment and pleasure. The Kama Sutra urges men to be well-dressed and to take care of their bodies which are both ways of relaxing. Receiving massages and attending to their beauty are ways in which men can switch off work and attune to silence and peace. The text also encourages spending some time every morning in meditation, beginning the day with a ritual, a prayer, a mantra, or simply a few moments of silence. This enriches the spirit and prepares the mind for the day ahead.

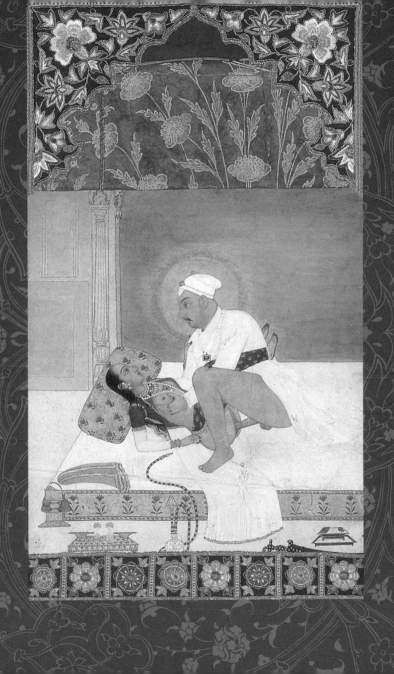

Meals should be taken regularly, preferably at the same time every day. In India, noon is the time of maximum heat, so it is suggested that lunch be eaten before the very hot hours, and then dinner after sunset, when it is cool again.

The Indian practice of teaching birds to speak is very ancient: Birds were considered sacred companions, and the species able to imitate human language were used to carry love messages between men and women, or to deliver important communication during battles and wars. Birds were companions in games and in secret intrigues, and they were kept in cages in the home or garden.

The late afternoon and evening is dedicated to friends, music, and poetry, and to engaging with beautiful women. In India evening receptions can sometimes go on all night; dancers and musicians entertain the host and his friends, including wives and girlfriends. This is a way of relaxing and replenishing one's life. The day is for working and the night is for playing, thus bringing balance and wholeness into the week. Traditionally, gatherings include a variety of guests, from scholars and poets to singers, entertainers, historians, and specialists in legendary epics. The elegant reception is cultural, where literature and history are discussed, music is played and poetry is read. Spending the evening hours in this way relaxes us and makes us better disposed toward love. When the man returns to his bedroom and begins the rituals of love he will have switched off completely from work and will be more attentive to his lover, focusing all his energies on her.

SUITABLE LOVERS

The sacred books recommend marriage within the same caste
—Brahman with Brahman, Kshatriya with Kshatriya—
and marriage to a virgin. Marriages to partners of one's own milieu
are more successful. After the birth of children, one is free. Kama can
then be practiced with other women according to certain rules:
not with women of higher castes or with married women of the same caste,

> *with some exceptions. The texts recommend sexual union with women*
> *of lower castes, with those who were once married but are now separated,*
> *widows, young girls, and prostitutes. Kama can be practiced with*
> *a married woman if she is of free will and has had other lovers, if she is*
> *about to separate from her husband, or if she has fallen in love with you.*
> —1.5 INTERMEDIARIES AND LOVERS

Once children are born, the Kama Sutra suggests that one is free to practice the erotic arts outside of marriage. However, there are rules set so as not to endanger the marriage and the well being of the children. One should choose lovers from social milieus other than one's own, thus keeping extramarital affairs separate from the family. Young girls, widows, and divorced women are all suitable, and women of one's own social set are suitable only if they have an open marriage—similarly, if they are about to separate from their husbands, have had other lovers, or have hopelessly fallen in love with you.

THE GO-BETWEEN

> *A man who is a common friend of both the man and his lover,*
> *and is trusted particularly by her, can become the go-between*
> *and the love messenger. He should have these qualities:*
> *Skillfulness*
> *A pushy and bold nature*
> *Insight*
> *Confidence*
> *Knowledge of other people's thinking*
> *A sense of doing things at the appropriate time and place*
> *Decisiveness in moments of crisis*
> *Easy and quick comprehension of situations and people*
> *Resourcefulness*
> *Speed at applying remedies*
> —1.5 INTERMEDIARIES AND LOVERS

A good friend is one's best psychologist and he or she will comprehend the delicacy of embarking on an affair. A male love messenger will be more assertive than the woman herself in encouraging her to taking the bold step of adultery. The love messenger needs to be someone who can keep secrets, someone who understands the deep yearnings of human nature that cannot be answered in conventional relationships. The go-between is perhaps the wisest person of the three, because he or she will encourage and yet act as the safety boundary for the two clandestine lovers. The love messenger will also listen to both and will guide them in their relationship, thus taking an active role of support and counseling. The Kama Sutra encourages us to choose our go-betweens with great care, and to bestow this role only upon the most trusted of friends.

Thus ends the first and most theoretical part of the Kama Sutra. It gives us the foundation of love. Living with elegance and refinement, playing the games of seduction with intelligence and insight, knowing the basis of our attractions—these are the essential, initiatory steps in the practice of the erotic arts.

Making Love

Stimulation of erotic desire happens both physically and mentally. Desire is more than strong physical attraction: It is also fantasy born in the imagination and then played in reality. The Kama Sutra teaches us to recognize our sexual persona: who we are, how we function, what best fulfills our desires. Successful seductions are the result of understanding the game of love and knowing how to play by the rules. Lovemaking is both impulse and technique; there is nothing more thrilling than going to bed with someone who teases us with variety and is expert in the techniques of kissing, biting, scratching, penetration, and oral sex—and knows how to end beautifully.

THE SEXUAL MATCH

In order to play the erotic games of the Kama Sutra, men and women need to understand the size and shape of their lovers' sexual organs, their degree of sexual enjoyment, and the passion of their sexual impulse. Men are divided into three categories: the hare, the bull, and the stallion. Women are equally divided into three categories: the doe, the mare, and the elephant.

The hare man's penis is six fingers long. He is of small stature with small feet, buttocks, hands, and ears; a gentle voice; beautiful teeth; and a lively body. The bull man's penis is eight fingers long; he has a large neck, an impressive bearing, clear skin, and a round, solid stomach. He is always lucky. The stallion man's penis is twelve fingers long. He has elongated ears, and lips, a long head, thin body, thick hair, long fingers, a luminous look, and powerful thighs.

The doe woman has beautiful hair, a thin body, and golden skin; her organ is cold like the moon. She has a low voice and abundant hair. She eats little, her face is narrow, and her sexual secretions are unscented. The mare woman has a strong nose, strong thighs, and her organ is always hot. Her skin is clear, her belly small, her limbs regular, and her sexual secretions lightly scented. The elephant woman is tall and powerful, her skin is pink, and her body is strong and harmonious. Her organ is now cold, now hot, and her sexual secretions are strongly scented.

There are three equal unions between men and women and six unequal sexual matches.

EQUAL: *The Hare Man with the Doe Woman*
             The Bull Man with the Mare Woman
             The Stallion Man with the Elephant Woman
UNEQUAL: *The Hare Man with the Mare Woman*
             The Hare Man with the Elephant Woman
             The Bull Man with the Doe Woman
             The Bull Man with the Elephant Woman
             The Stallion Man with the Doe Woman
             The Stallion Man with the Mare Woman

Just as we consult horoscopes and enneagrams to find out about our lover's character, so we should spend time studying his or her sexual potential. Physical characteristics in ancient India were regarded as a reflection of the divine plan: lovers are beautiful together when they are completely matched, meant to melt into one another. If the man is too big for the woman, for instance, he will have to be careful with her, and she may hurt after their lovemaking. If the woman is too large for the man, she won't be able to achieve orgasm easily, and the walls of her vagina won't enclose his penis tightly enough for maximum pleasure. The Kama Sutra suggests positions and ways for "high and low congress," or lovemaking for unequal partners.

There are nine different types of unions according to the intensity of sexual desire and passion. A man is of small sexual desire when, at the time of lovemaking, he is not very passionate, doesn't exert himself much, and produces scanty semen. A man of stronger passion is called "middling," and a man of great passion is called "intense." Before entering into a sexual relationship, spend some time thinking about your sexual match. Is he going to match your passion? Is her husband satisfying her and will she thus have small or middling passion for you? Is he intense, and do you have the stamina to match him well? Thinking about the degree of desire is part of the preparation for erotic play, so that when you are making love you will gauge your partner's intensity and be able to moderate your techniques to suit the mood of the moment. These are the nine passion-matches:

MEN	WOMEN
Small	*Small*
Middling	*Middling*
Intense	*Intense*
Small	*Middling*
Small	*Intense*
Middling	*Small*
Middling	*Intense*
Intense	*Small*
Intense	*Middling*

A man whose activity lasts long pleases women, who complain about men
who reach orgasm quickly. In sexual union, the man's passion is intense
yet short-timed in the beginning. And that of woman is slow, gradual
and yet long-timed until her climax. But on subsequent sexual unions
the same day, the position is reversed. The woman's passion becomes
intense and short-lived, until she is finally satisfied.

—2.1 TYPES OF SEXUAL UNION ACCORDING TO TYPE AND DURATION

THE DIFFERENT KINDS OF LOVE

The Kama Sutra teaches that there are different kinds of love. We are
attracted to each other primarily because we are infatuated with the idea
of the other, of making love, and of the pleasures to be shared together.
Knowing the basis of our attraction is a good foundation to making the
perfect love match. There are four kinds of attractions:

LOVE BORN FROM PRACTICE

Practiced seduction through speech, gestures, manners, and skills
of the lover. Long practice is like the love of hunting for the hunter.
We can easily seduce because we know exactly how to play the game.

LOVE BORN FROM THE IMAGINATION

The anticipation of love, the dreams, the fantasies, the imagination
of what it will be like all carry a power that slowly seduces us into
the idea of being with another.

SUBSTITUTE LOVE

When we see a stranger that resembles someone we have loved in the
past, or reminds us of someone with whom we fell in love though we
could never act on it. An archetype has thus been awakened within
us, and the other is its personification.

LOVE BORN FROM THE PERCEPTION OF EXTERNAL OBJECTS

We see a man parachuting down from the sky and we immediately fall in love with him. Why? It is love clothed in the grand and heroic: a great car, wealth, an important job, or the right clothes can all stimulate us and work on our sexual fantasies—we fall in love with the person because of those objects.

EMBRACING

Four different types of embrace are part of the preliminaries of seduction. When we embrace someone we come close to them physically, but how we embrace them sends a variety of signals, some of which make explicit our sexual intentions.

Sprishtaka, OR TOUCHING EMBRACE

The man, under some pretext, goes in front or alongside a woman and brushes his body against hers.

Viddhaka, OR BRUISING EMBRACE

Discovering the man alone, the woman bends down as if to pick something up and thrusts against him, and he in turn takes hold of her and embraces her lightly.

Uddhrishtaka, OR BARING EMBRACE

The man and the woman, while walking in the dark or being alone in a room, touch or brush their bodies together and then embrace, undressing each other enough to caress bare skin.

Piditaka, OR SQUEEZING EMBRACE

Either the man or the woman presses the other's body firmly against a wall or pillar and moves sensuously against it.

These embraces are for couples who have not yet made love, but are still in the stages of seduction. There are four more passionate types of embraces to be practiced by lovers who have made love.

Lataveshtitaka, OR ENCIRCLING LIKE A LIANA
The woman entwines herself around the man like a creeper to a tree. Pulling his face down to hers, she kisses him lightly, making soft love sounds.

Vrikshadhirudhaka, OR CLIMBING THE TREE
The woman, having placed one foot on the man's foot and pressing the other against his thigh, passes an arm behind his back, and places the other on his shoulder. She utters small pleasure cries and climbs up to him for kissing.

Tilatandulaka, OR SESAME AND RICE
The man and the woman lie on their sides in bed, and embrace each other in such a way that their arms and legs are completely entwined, like grains of rice mixed with seeds of sesame.

Kshiranira, OR MILK AND WATER
Full of passion and unable to wait, the man and woman embrace—either lying face to face, or with the woman sitting on the man's lap —and press against each other with great desire.

KISSING

The Kama Sutra enumerates a science of kissing: in different ways, on different parts of the body, and for different moods, from modest to passionate.

Nimittaka, OR NOMINAL KISS
The woman is pulled against the man for the first time and his mouth presses against hers, but she doesn't return his kiss in order to arouse his passion with her reluctance.

Sfuritaka, OR THROBBING KISS
The woman returns the man's kiss by moving and pressing her lower lip without moving the upper one.

Sama, OR STRAIGHT KISS
The lips of the two lovers are brought into straight and direct contact with each other.

Tiryaka, OR SLANTED KISS
One of the two lovers presses his or her lips against those of the other at an angle.

Udabhranta, OR TURNED KISS
One of the two lovers stands behind the other and turns up the lover's face, kissing him or her while holding the head and chin.

Avapiditaka, OR PRESSED KISS
The above three kisses practiced with passion and pressure.

Panchama Grabana, OR THE FIFTH HOLD KISS
One of the lovers holds the other's cheeks between his or her hands and presses their lips together, slowly opening into a kiss.

THE KISSING GAME

This is a game to be repeated over and over. The first to seize the other's lower lip is the winner. As in all games, it is necessary to catch the other by surprise. The loser will then initiate a stimulating quarrel and demand that the game be started again. The losing lover should then take hold of the other's lower lip and bite it gently, never letting go of it. The game can continue like this to the lovers' delight.

Uttarachumban, OR RETURN KISS
The man kisses the woman's upper lip and she in turn kisses his lower lip.

Samputaka, OR CLASPING KISS
The man sucks the woman's lips and probes with his tongue to open her mouth.

Jihvayuddha OR THE FIGHTING OF THE TONGUE
He runs his tongue on her teeth and palate.

The art of kissing can be practiced in four different modes:

Sama, OR BALANCED MODE
Facing each other lying down or sitting, the lovers kiss each other's thighs, chests, and sides.

Pidita, OR FORCING MODE
Breasts, cheeks, navels, and buttocks are kissed, pressed, and pricked.

Anchita, OR THE SOFT TOUCH
The skin below the breasts is kissed and caressed at the same time.

Mridu, OR GENTLE MODE
Kissing on the forehead or eyes.

To arouse his passion, a woman should kiss her lover while he is sleeping.
Upon waking, feeling her intentions, he will be ready to make love.
This kiss is called Ragadipana, or Kiss That Kindles Love.

When a man is busy at work, when he is quarreling with his lover,
or when his attention is diverted to something else—or, worse, he's falling
asleep—the woman should kiss him gently in order to divert his attention
toward her, and this kiss is called Chalitakam, or Kiss That Turns Away.

When a man returns home late at night, he kisses the sleeping woman,
arousing her passion. This kiss is called Pratibodhakam, or Kiss That Awakens.

When a lover kisses the reflection of his beloved in a mirror or on water,
it is called Chhayachumbana, or Kiss of the Shadow.

When a man kisses a woman's child, or an image of her,
it is called Sankrantak, or Transference Kiss.

When a woman massages the man's body and rests her face on his thigh,
it is called Uruchumbana, or Demonstrative Kiss.

—2.3 ON KISSING

SCRATCHING

It is impossible to list the innumerable nail-markings lovers may make on each other's bodies at the height of passion. The Kama Sutra lists a few scratching and marking techniques that remain imprinted on the skin for a few days after a lovers' encounter, as small mementos of passion.

The places for nail marks are the armpits, the breasts, the buttocks, the throat, the back, the thighs, and the thigh joints. Marks on the private parts make a woman remember anew her date and lovemaking with her lover.
—2.4 ON MARKING WITH THE NAILS

When passion is intense, lovers may practice these types of scratching:

Acchuritaka, OR LIMITED PRESSURE
Keeping the fingers close together, the cheek, the breasts, and the lower lips are scratched so gently that no mark is left but only the body hair stands up out of thrill.

Ardhachandra, OR HALF-MOON
Nail marks made on the neck or breasts in the form of the crescent moon.

Mandala, OR CIRCULAR
Two half-moons facing each other are called Mandala. They are made on the navel, on the hips, and the joints of the thighs.

Rekha, OR LINEAR
Linear marks can be made on any part of the body, but they should not be large.

Vyaghranakha, OR TIGER'S CLAW
Linear marks made with five fingers so that they curve around the nipple.

Mayurapadaka, OR PEACOCK'S FOOT
The same line as the Tiger's Claw is made with five nails in the shape of a peacock's foot.

Shashaplutaka, OR JUMPING HARE
Five nail marks are made close together , in the shape of a jumping hare, near the nipple.

Utpalapatraka, OR LOTUS PETAL
Nail marks on the breasts and waist resembling the petals of a lotus flower.

If there are no nail marks on the body of the woman to remind her of love,
youth, and beauty, then the love not practiced for long is ruined forever.
Even when a stranger observes the nail-marked breasts of a young woman
from a distance he is imbued with love and respect for her.
—2.4 ON MARKING WITH THE NAILS

BITING

Biting, yet another game of love, can be extremely sexy. The Kama Sutra teaches that except for the delicate areas of the upper lip, the tongue, and the eyes, all other parts of the body are fit for biting.

Gudhaka, OR HIDDEN BITE
The lower lip is pressed with teeth so gently that no mark is left.

Uchchhunaka, OR SWOLLEN BITE
The lower lip is bitten with pressure.

Bindu, OR POINT BITE
A small portion of the lower lip is bitten with two teeth.

Bidumala, OR LINE OF POINTS
Small portions of the skin are bitten with all the teeth.

CORAL BITE
The bite practiced again and again with teeth and lips in one place.

Manimala, OR LINE OF JEWELS
The Coral Bite is practiced in many places in a row.

Khandabhraka, OR BROKEN CLOUD
Teeth marks resembling broken clouds are made on the breasts.

Varahcharvita, OR BOAR BITING
Close, continuous, and slightly red teeth markings.

Embracing, kissing, scratching, and biting are detailed in their sequence.
They all increase passion, and each succeeding one is more intense.
When the man and woman thus indulge in the Kama Sutra way of lovemaking,
their love shall not be lessened even in a hundred years.
—2.5 ON BITING

POSITIONS

Because of the different types of men and women, the Kama Sutra gives
general positions for lovemaking and suggestions for variations to be
adopted by unequal partners.

When a Doe Woman has sex with a Bull Man,
she should lie down on her back with her legs far apart in order to open for him.
On the other hand, an Elephant Woman having sex with a Hare Man
contracts in order to increase their pleasure.
When a man and woman of similar dimensions unite,

the woman should lie down in a natural position.
If the man's penis is too small and he will not be able to satisfy her,
she should use dildos to gratify her passion.
—2.6 COPULATION

The Kama Sutra directs a woman to dilate when making love to a man of superior caliber, and to contract for a man of inferior caliber. Sex with a man of equal type is effortless. When looking for the perfect dildo, the woman should choose one that matches her exactly.

The following three postures are the best for a woman who needs to dilate for her partner:

Utphallaka, OR BLOSSOMING
The woman's head is lowered and her back and hips are raised, stretching the entrance of her vagina wide. A pillow should be placed beneath her back. After every stroke, the man should withdraw a little and then suddenly thrust long and fully.

Vijrimbhitaka, OR OPENING
The woman raises her thighs and keeps them wide apart.

Indrani, OR THE CONSORT OF INDRA
Indra is the Hindu god of the lower deities. Encircling the woman's thighs and keeping his knees at her side, the man widens her as he penetrates. This position requires practice.

The next three positions are ideal for the woman who needs to contract her vagina for her partner:

Samputaka, OR CLASPING
When the woman and the man lie face to face on their sides, the position is called Lateral Clasping. The man should always lie to the

right of the woman, she should always be to his left. When the woman is lying down and the man is stretched on top of her it is called the Closed Clasping (this is commonly known as the "missionary" position).

Piditaka, OR PRESSING
In the Clasping position, the man penetrates the woman urgently.

Veshtitaka, OR TWINING
When making love in the Clasping position, the woman places her left leg on the right in order to contract her vagina even more.

There are other positions that lovers should try for variety and to increase their pleasure.

Vadavaka, OR THE MARE
The woman holds the man's penis inside her vagina without touching him or caressing him in any way. He penetrates her again and again just by thrusting into her without any other movement.

Bhugnaka, OR BENT
The woman holds both her legs high in the air.

Jrimbhitaka, OR GAPING
The woman places both her legs over the man's shoulders.

Utpiditaka, OR HIGH PRESSURE
The woman folds her legs and places them against the man's chest. Every time he penetrates he presses against her.

Ardhapiditaka, OR HALF-PRESSED
The woman only folds one leg against the man's chest.

Venudaritaka, OR BROKEN BAMBOO
The woman places one leg on the man's shoulder and stretches
the other out.

Shulachitaka, OR IMPALEMENT
The woman places her foot on the man's head and stretches the other
leg out, then alternates the position. This requires much practice.

Karkata, OR CRAB
Like a crab folding its claws, the woman bends her legs and the man
penetrates her, pressing his navel against her legs.

Piditaka, OR TIGHT
The woman crosses her raised legs.

Padmasana, OR LOTUS
The woman folds her legs in the lotus position.

Paravrittaka, OR THE SPIN
Embracing the woman who is lying with her back to him, the man
turns her around without withdrawing from her.

These positions can be practiced lying down, sitting, or standing. One of
the best places to experiment with new positions is in water, making love
in a Jacuzzi, a hot tub, or in the sea at night. Gravity is lessened and the
lovers can experiment freely with new ways of making love.

A man should increase and experiment with the ways of lovemaking,
as this will increase and enhance the lovers' passion and mutual attraction.
A man who pleases his woman with sexual variety is intensely loved,
liked, and respected by women.

—2.6 COPULATION

STRIKING AND LOVE SOUNDS

Little blows and love sounds are greatly arousing during lovemaking. Sex can sometimes be so passionate as to resemble a battle between lovers. Gentle blows are one of the main means of arousing passion. The Kama Sutra has wisely delineated the different kinds of blows and love sounds that are most exciting for lovers.

The shoulders, the space between the breasts, the back, the thighs, the head, and the sides are all good places for striking. The gentle blows can be of four kinds:

Striking With the Back of the Hand
Striking With Contracted Fingers
Striking With the Fist
Striking With the Open Palm

Women sing or cry out during sex and their sounds can excite a man as much as the act of penetration itself. There are eight kinds of love sounds:

The *Hin* sound starts from the throat and mounts through the nostrils in a high, light, and fast note.
The Roll of Thunder begins as a "ha" deep in the throat.
The Hissing Sound comes with fast and shallow penetration.
The Weeping Sound is like a rolling cry.
The Sighing Sound is a drawing in of the breath.
The Cry of Pain comes when penetration is deep.
The Violent Outbreath is the sound of great pleasure.

REVERSAL OF ROLES AND THE RHYTHMS OF PENETRATION

Women's capacity for orgasm is greater than men's, and they are slower to reach the height of passion. If the man needs to rest after lovemaking, one of the games the Kama Sutra suggests for the lovers is that of role reversal. Observing the way the woman seduces him and penetrates him with a dildo teaches the man something about her, the way she would like to be seduced and penetrated. In this game the lovers learn each other's deep, secret yearnings.

When the woman finds her man fatigued and she is not yet satisfied, she may, with his permission, act his role. Even when the man is not fatigued, she may switch roles for the sake of novelty and to satisfy the curiosity of the man. She can turn around and get on top of him, and continues lovemaking by descending on his anus with the aid of an accessory, imposing her idea of virile behavior on him. When the man is lying down and listening to her amorous talk, she should loosen his underclothes, and when his penis is erect she should caress him gently, especially the insides of his thighs.

—2.8 ABOUT WOMEN ACTING THE ROLE OF MEN

Women can also play role reversal with each other, either alone or in the presence of a man.

The woman lays her hands upon her partner's breasts, pressing them, and feels her armpits, sides, neck, and thighs before undoing her clothes. Then, taking hold of her lover's hair, the woman should kiss her. Seizing hold of her lover's pubic hair, the woman kisses her pubis, slipping her finger inside her vagina. These parts of the body should be pressed again and again, and the lover will turn her eyes overwhelmed with pleasure. This makes a woman's passion rouse easily, and it is a great secret of women's ways.

—2.8 ABOUT WOMEN ACTING THE ROLE OF MEN

The Kama Sutra outlines ten rhythms of penetration and suggests that the man adopt several during each lovemaking session to delight his partner with increasing modes of passion.

NORMAL COPULATION
Straight penetration, when the penis enters the vagina normally and gently.

CHURNING
The man holds the penis with his hand and turns it round and round inside the vagina.

THE ROD
Bending the woman and penetrating her from behind, the penis enters the lowered vagina at a higher angle.

THE DEVASTATOR
In the same backward position, the vagina is raised and the penis penetrates violently from the top downwards.

THE CRUEL
The penis is driven in fully and pressed in for some time before withdrawing.

THE THUNDERBOLT
The penis is withdrawn to some distance and then let fall into the vagina with some force.

THE WILD BOAR'S THRUST
Thrusting on only one side of the vagina.

THE BULL'S ATTACK
Thrusting now on one side, now on the other, like the horns of a bull.

THE BIRD'S AMUSEMENT
Without withdrawing his penis, the man thrusts again and again in increasing frequency. This marks his culmination, because this is the rhythm that drives him to orgasm.

THE CLASPING
When the penis doesn't move at all inside the vagina and the lovers press against each other.

In addition to the ten strokes above, the man and the woman, reversing roles, can use three types of movement to increase each other's pleasure:

THE PINCHING
The woman squeezes the penis tightly and for a long time.

THE BEE
Lifting her body with her hands and folding her legs to support herself, the woman holds the penis in her vagina and turns it round and round.

THE SWING
The woman swings her hips and abdomen in a circular motion or from side to side.

> *When the woman is fatigued, she should rest*
> *by placing her forehead on that of the man,*
> *still keeping him inside her. Then, having rested herself,*
> *the man should begin intercourse afresh.*
> —2.8 ABOUT WOMEN ACTING THE ROLE OF MEN

ORAL SEX

Cunnilingus and fellatio are included in the Kama Sutra because they are expressions of the erotic instinct, but they are condemned as unholy. In fact, practicing fellatio or cunnilingus with one's wife "destroys fifteen years of the celestial life of the husband's ancestors." Oral sex is practiced by eunuchs, male and female prostitutes, people of lower castes, and foreigners. The Kama Sutra does not discount that lovers may on occasion —and secretly—experiment with fellatio and cunnilingus, but it is recommended that such practices be avoided. However, the text lists eight kinds of fellatio:

Nimitta, OR CASUAL
Clasping the penis with one hand, the lips are placed gently on the mast while pressing, releasing, and shaking.

Parshvatodashta, OR NIBBLING THE SIDES
Covering the end of the penis with fingers gathered like a flower, the woman nibbles the sides gently and then softens her bite.

Bahihsandamsha, OR EXTERNAL PINCHING
Taking the end of the penis in her mouth, the woman presses it with her lips, sucking and kissing.

Antahsandamsha, OR INTERNAL PINCHING
Drawing the penis further into her mouth, the woman kisses it, causing an ejaculation.

Chumbitaka, OR KISSING
Holding the penis with her hands, the woman kisses it with passion.

Parimrishtaka, OR BROWSING
The woman tickles the penis with the tip of her tongue, licking the mast and titillating the opening.

Amrachushitaka, OR SUCKING THE MANGO
Without holding the mast, the woman draws half or more of the penis into her mouth, and sucks it with passion as though she were sucking on a mango.

Sangara, OR DEVOURING
Putting the penis in her mouth as far as it will go, she sucks until he orgasms.

According to the Kama Sutra, cunnilingus is only occasionally practiced by men and women, but is more usual between women. Men and women can play in the Crow position, known to us as Sixty-Nine.

> *In some cases, in some places, for some people, on some occasions,*
> *oral sex may not be bad; rather, it may prove useful and satisfactory.*
> *A man should therefore give due consideration to place, time,*
> *the practice to be engaged in, and its agreeability, and then decide*
> *whether to do or not do a certain thing.*
>
> —2.9 ON ORAL SEX

THE BEGINNING AND ENDING OF LOVEMAKING

The time before and after making love has an essential, especially touching quality. The Kama Sutra places special emphasis on these moments when lovers bond and fall in love with each other.

In his home, decorated with flowers and made fragrant with burning incense, the well-bred citizen should receive the woman after he has bathed, dressed elegantly, and drunk a little. Sitting by her side he should invite her to drink. He should sit on her right, touch her hair tenderly, touch her clothes and gently undress her, and with his left hand slowly prepare her for lovemaking. They should indulge in amorous conversation on various subjects, and talk suggestively of secret things between them that cannot be mentioned in a gathering. Then, surrounded by music, he should converse on fine arts, offer drinks, and arouse her passion. He should then welcome her by offering small presents. Once he sees that her passion is fully aroused, he should make sure that they are absolutely alone in the home. After this, in the privacy of his bedroom, he should continue with his embraces, and kissing her, he should gently undress her. Such are the actions to be performed before lovemaking.

After lovemaking and being fully satisfied, the lovers should go into separate bathrooms and recompose themselves. They then should sit in a place different from where they made love and perhaps eat some sweet fruit, soup, juice, mango fruit, lemon slices with sugar, or anything else that is sweet and pure. Seating themselves on the roof, if the season so favors, they may enjoy the moonlight, and indulge in pleasant conversation. The woman should lie down on her lover's lap, gazing at the loveliness of the moon, and he should show her the different constellations and planets. Then, calm in mind and body, they should retire to sleep in separate beds.

The mutual dalliance, the embracing, the kissing, the exchange of tenderness are sure ways of rekindling passion. Expressions of loving feelings remove anger and anxiety and renew the bond. Dances, songs, the joyous reminiscence of the first time, and details of the pangs of separation all heighten passion and increase love.

India is a country where people marry very young, and are still often betrothed to one another by their families and marriages are arranged during childhood. Being attracted to people we are not married to is very natural, but such feelings can sometimes take the form of deep longings and mental obsessions. The Kama Sutra counsels wisely on what to do when our passions are hopelessly aroused by someone who is married, and suggests that before we embark on an affair we carefully examine whether the other person is accessible, what risks are involved in the situation, what the consequences of the affair would be, and whether it should be embarked on at all. If, after examining the situation carefully, we still feel we cannot exist without winning over the other person, then we should try to make love and see if our hunger can be satisfied in one encounter. The Kama Sutra offers no judgment against adulterous relationships, because it studies the nature of people as they are, not as they should behave by some moral standard. If the affair is conducted discreetly and in a way that brings no harm to anyone, it can often be a bounty of happiness and joy in situations when partners no longer love each other or don't get on. In the following passages we will see that the Kama Sutra intimates that it is the man who should take the initiative in the seduction of a married woman. In a contemporary context, these ancient Kama Sutra rules can be interpreted as appropriate for either man or woman, as they force us to reflect deeply and carefully on the nature, ways, and consequences of the affair before we allow it to happen.

The Kama Sutra delineates ten stages of adulterous passion:

1. *Love at First Sight*
2. *Mental Obsession*
3. *Constant Infatuation*
4. *Loss of Sleep*
5. *Loss of Weight*
6. *Indifference to Everything in Life*
7. *Loss of Mental and Spiritual Balance*
8. *Madness*
9. *Fainting Fits*
10. *Death*

—5.1 ON THE CHARACTERISTICS OF MEN AND
WOMEN INFATUATED WITH ANOTHER

From the first glance our passion can be aroused exponentially and cause deep us suffering, madness, fainting fits, and even death. If we find ourselves displaying one or more of the ten symptoms the Kama Sutra guides us in considering the situation carefully. The priests of Kama Sutra say that those who are skilled in the art of the affair can from the very beginning judge whether a man or woman is virtuous, or whether he or she likes to flirt. The person's appearance and physical features can tell us a lot about whether he or she would entertain the idea of an adulterous relationship. A person's conduct, feelings, and expressions give us further clues as to whether an affair would ever be possible. Handsome and good men attract women, and beautiful women attract men all the time, but they may never proceed further than a subtle acknowledgment of their passion. The Kama Sutra suggests however that when a woman falls in love she has no regard for right or wrong, and if she shrinks from the advances of a man initially, she will capitulate if he persists. A lot of men, on the other hand, will subdue their feelings and never enter into an adulterous relationship with a married woman no matter how much she may want

them. The Kama Sutra also warns that when a woman commits adultery she is likely to want the relationship to progress, whereas men may turn indifferent after the first time because the conquest was the exciting element of the passion.

The Kama Sutra lists twenty-four reasons why a woman may not entertain an affair:

1. *She loves her husband.*
2. *She loves her children.*
3. *There has been sorrow or bereavement in the family.*
4. *There is no opportunity for her to free herself.*
5. *If she is not approached elegantly, she becomes angry.*
6. *She suspects that the adulterous relationship won't go anywhere.*
7. *She fears that he has a lover already.*
8. *She fears that he cannot keep secrets.*
9. *She fears he will tell his friends.*
10. *She is concerned that he is too powerful and famous.*
11. *She suspects he is just playing.*
12. *A Doe Woman fears that the man may be too large for her and use violent thrusts while making love.*
13. *She is concerned that she may not be as skilled as he in the erotic arts of the Kama Sutra and may feel inadequate.*
14. *He has been a close friend before.*
15. *He lacks financial means.*
16. *He is of low status.*
17. *He fails to respond to her emotionally.*
18. *She is an Elephant Woman and she discovers that he is a Hare Man who will not satisfy her sexually.*
19. *She is concerned that some harm may come to him if they start an affair.*
20. *She is concerned about her physical defects.*
21. *She fears that their affair will be discovered and that she will be divorced.*
22. *She finds the man too old.*

23. *She suspects that her husband has set her up by asking*
    a friend to seduce her to test the extent of her commitment.
24. *Religious considerations ultimately prevent her from*
    embarking on the affair.

If the man is set on initiating the seduction of a married woman he must skillfully remove any of the above fears or concerns from the very beginning, and, as a way of convincing her, increase his passionate pursuit. Moral objections, pride, and self-respect tend to dissolve when her passion is engaged. Friendship is a good way of getting close to her and she is likely to feel less threatened when the friendship turns into an erotic interest. In matters of infidelity, the first step is to establish a relationship of trust: the woman must feel that he is not going to make any mistakes in his conduct with her, and he must ensure that her fears don't turn into obstacles to their passion.

By knowing how to skillfully navigate the circumstances surrounding the beginning of the affair and in controlling his behavior to remove all obstacles, the man can be successful in his conquest. The Kama Sutra counsels that there are certain qualities in a man that women highly appreciate and that these should be studied and become second-nature to any man who wants to be successful in his seduction techniques:

He is well versed in the erotic arts of the Kama Sutra; he is a master storyteller; has known the woman for a long time. He appears to be young and yet mature, is good at sports, pays attention to her demands, talks well and sweetly, gives her gifts, and has given her the opportunity to obtain information on him by a trusted go-between. Beautiful women already desire him. He knows her secrets and weaknesses, and he has met her secretly before. He is famous and charming. He is a neighbor or has been brought up with her. He knows the arts of love and is devoted to pleasure. He has some family or friendship tie to her. He is a lover of music and theatre. He has traveled the world. He is generous in his gifts. His health is vibrant, and he is courageous and fearless, excelling her husband in

looks, learning, merits, and in the knowledge of the erotic arts. He dresses
smartly and is sexually extremely attractive.
—5.1 ON MEN WHO ARE SUCCESSFUL WITH THEIR WOMEN

These are qualities that appeal to all women, but not all married women will have affairs. Affairs seldom happen by chance, and we entertain infidelity when our main relationship or marriage is unsatisfying. The Kama Sutra suggests that the man consider why a woman may be open to having an affair and study the circumstances in her marriage or main relationship. Women who display the following characteristics may be easily won over:

She stands on her doorstep and looks longingly at life passing by.
She looks away flirtatiously when he looks at her.
She dislikes her husband.
She is a flirt.
She is childless.
She still lives with her parents.
She is a gossip and her friendships are superficial.
She is the wife of a performing artist often away.
She is a very young widow.
She loves luxury despite her poverty.
She is proud of her beauty and her husband is of low social status.
She is vain and proud of her skills and is bored by her husband.
She finds other men more interesting than her husband.
She is equal to her husband in intelligence, knowledge,
*   and strength of character.*
Her partner for no good reason humiliates her.
She is married to someone who is often away.
She is married to someone with many brothers or
*   is not well regarded by the other women in the family.*

The Kama Sutra suggests that these women will look elsewhere for sexual satisfaction. It is entirely natural for men and women to be attracted and in attempting to establish a relationship skill must be used so that feelings become explicit and the passion quickly becomes an obsession. This is the time to make love and begin the affair. The Chandogya Upanishad, an ancient sacred scripture, describes adulterous relationships as following a kind of celestial order that satisfies deep longings: "…the woman's call is the prelude, lying with her is the hymn, penetrating her is the offer, and ejaculating inside her is the final hymn." These are sacred hymns that lead to happiness: "For the man who puts these hymns into practice, such coupling is fruitful. The man becomes more active, he lives his whole life, he prospers in children, cattle, and fame. He has numerous lovers; he abandons no one, if such is his vow. This means he never abandons a woman who has shared his bed." Vatsyayana was writing rules of love and erotic practice that could be inspiring for everyone, across cultures, and across cycles of time with different moral rules.

The crux of the affair is trust. Trust is needed to break the rules and to experiment with feelings and sexuality with someone other than our main partner. The Kama Sutra wisely counsels that trust is won over time and begins in seed form as friendship that can eventually blossom into an erotic affair. The best way to approach the person we are interested in is on our own, but if there are difficulties in doing so, the Kama Sutra suggests we use a trusted go-between to melt the ice initially. If the woman agrees to an initial meeting, then the man should speak boldly of his feelings for her and make his intentions explicit; if she makes difficulties, then it may be the go-between's job to convince her. Meetings are of two kinds: natural and attempted. Natural meetings are when we bump into the other person and naturally seek some seclusion where feelings can be discussed openly, knowing that no one is listening or watching. Attempted meetings are when we deliberately make an effort to meet the other at some party, or at a place we know they are going to be, and then steer them towards a corner where we can be alone.

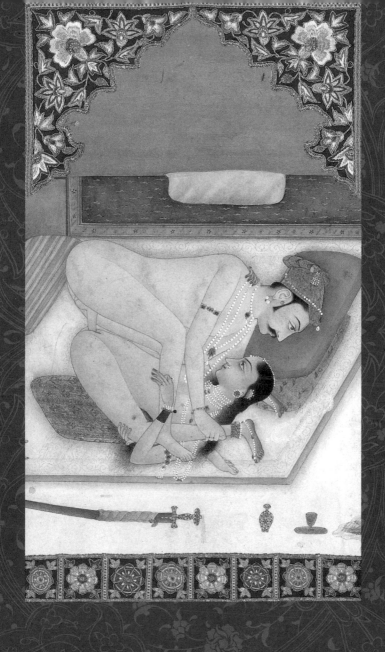

When a man meets his desired woman he should gaze at her,
and observe her smallest gestures. When she looks at him and people
surround them, he talks to his friends about her, teasing her all the time.
If he is sitting next to another woman, he shows signs of boredom and
indifference towards her. He should always speak with her children
and show her that he cares for them. He makes friends with someone close
to her and conveys his feelings of adoration. He tries to see her
whenever possible to win her confidence. He has jewelry she likes
specially made for her by the goldsmith, the jeweler, and often
brings her wonderful flower arrangements. In her presence he discusses
the Kama Sutra but pretending it is not specifically about her.
With constant attention over time, he ends up being accepted.
Once they become more intimate, he leaves small mementos with her,
and tries to help her in any way she may need so as to appear
a friend and disguise his true feelings from others. He discusses interesting
topics with her and talks of ancient customs and practices with her servants,
always agreeing and praising her for her wisdom and intelligence.
—5.2 ON MAKING THE ACQUAINTANCE OF A WOMAN
AND THE EFFORTS TO WIN HER OVER

Having become this close, the two make love and follow the rules of
seduction and lovemaking listed in previous parts of the book. The first
time should be long, beautiful, and satisfying. He should not make love to
her twice, but leave her hungry and wanting more. Once sexual relations
have begun, the lovers exchange gifts and share each other's things,
increasing their closeness. They meet in secret places and there they kiss,
caress each other's bodies, and make love undisturbed. With repeated
encounters an indestructible relationship is established between them that
can overcome any future obstacles to their passion. A wise man will have
an affair with a woman with whom a long relationship can be established,
not with someone too suspicious by nature, too timid, or overprotected
by her family.

The Kama Sutra subtly articulates the language of adulterous love and gives suggestions on how to establish an affair that will bring happiness and satisfaction to both lovers, without harming anyone. Through gifts, attention, the art of listening, making feelings explicit, and winning trust and confidence in one another, the lovers know each other as friends first and then as sexual partners. They must then find a place for their love encounters where they can be alone and not raise suspicions. Unless they can meet in the home of a trusted go-between, the Kama Sutra suggests eight other places for lovemaking: fields, gardens, ruined temples, an abandoned courtyard, a caravansary, cemeteries, or the banks of a river. Nature is often the perfect canopy for love and has her own special way of protecting our most forbidden passions.

The Benefits of the Kama Sutra

Vatsyayana composed the Kama Sutra for the well-being of the individual and for the comfort of society. When men and women are nurtured, loved, and happy in healthy relationships, the whole society becomes stable and prospers. He collected the essence of ancient holy works and composed a text that has been studied and followed for many centuries by people all over the world. The Kama Sutra is the ultimate teaching of the rules of love and erotic practice, and Vatsyayana's aim was not to spread lust but to encourage us to deepen our understanding of our own sexuality and to cultivate the erotic arts with elegance and refinement.

The Pandits of Dharma, Artha, and Kama hold these
sixty-four arts in great respect and as a means of protecting women.
Courtesans revere these arts as the means of their livelihood
Even when the cunning respect them for their usefulness,
what man will not worship these noble arts?
The sixty-four arts should be welcomed by every well-bred citizen.
The priests have defined these arts as respected,
charming, benevolent, and so dear to women.
A man who is skilled in the sixty-four arts is looked upon
with great honor by girls, remarried women, wives of other men, courtesans,
and all other women as well. A good lover is their hero.
—2.10 HOW TO BEGIN AND END LOVEMAKING

Bibliography

Burton, Richard. *The Illustrated Kama Sutra * Ananga Ranga * Perfumed Garden: The Classic Eastern Love Text*. Rochester, VT: Inner Traditions, 1991.

Danièlou, Alain. *The Complete Kama Sutra*. Rochester, VT: Park Street Press, 1994.

Halu, Zen and Misha. *Kama Sutra: The Arts of Love*. London: Thorsons Penguin, 1994.

Hooper, Anna. *Kama Sutra: Classic Lovemaking Techniques Reinterpreted for Today's Lovers*. London: Dorling Kindersley, 1994.

Mathur, Asharani. *Kama Sutra*. Mumbai, India: India Book Distributor, 1994.

Pichard, Georges. *The Illustrated Kama Sutra*. New York: NBM Publishing, 1991.

Further Reading List

Comfort, Alex. *Koka Shastra: Medieval Indian Writings on Love Based on the Kama Sutra.* New York: Simon & Schuster, 1997.

Vatsyayana. *Kama Sutra.* Mumbai, India: Nesma Books, 1999.

Vatsyayana. Indra Sinha, trans. *The Love Teachings of Kama Sutra: With Extracts from Koka Shastra, Ananga Ranga, and Other Famous Indian Works on Love.* London: Marlowe & Co, 1999.

Acknowledgments

Thank you to Bhikkhu and Waduda of New Earth Records for suggesting
an idea that was but a dream. My thanks also go to the wonderful team at
Harmony who made this project possible: Chip Gibson, Linda Loewenthal,
and Kieran O'Brien. A heartfelt thank you to my editor, Patricia Gift,
whose friendship and guidance continues to bring happy authors and good
projects to her list. Thank you to Marc Thorpe for the wonderful skill
of bringing the Khajuraho temple alive in this statue. Thank you to Julie
Foakes for finding the rare and stunning images to adorn this book and
box. Finally, without you Bullet, none of this would be possible. And a
wave of deep devotion to P, always there, always so loving.

Box art, left spine: Man climbing up to woman's window, © The British
Museum, London. *Insert on left spine:* Carving from an ivory panel
showing a couple making love, private collection, Werner Forman
Archive, London. *Right spine:* Sleeping woman, © Victoria & Albert
Museum, London. *Top panel*: Detail from a painting showing Krishna on
a tree, watching the Gopis bathing, © Victoria & Albert Museum, London.
Bottom panel: Detail from the same painting, showing the Gopis bathing
being watched by Krishna up on the tree, © Victoria & Albert Museum,
London. *Back of box:* Couple wrapped in quilt, © ET Archive, London.

Book jacket, insert: Woman combing her hair, © Victoria & Albert
Museum, London.

Book cover, front and back: Carving from an ivory panel showing a
couple making love, private collection, Werner Forman Archive, London.

Title page: An Indian album painting from the late 18th century, private collection, Werner Forman Archive, London.

Page 6: Internal courtyard from the women's quarters, © ET Archive, London.

Page 8: Krishna painting Radha's toenails, © ET Archive, London.

Page 10: Detail of the carvings from the Khajuraho erotic temple complex in India, Richard Weller, © Ardea, London.

Page 12: Couple making love, © The British Museum, London.

Page 14: An Indian album painting from late 18th century showing a couple making love, private collection, Werner Forman Archive, London.

Page 18: Erotic scene from an 18th century Indian manuscript of the Kama Sutra, ET Archive, London.

Page 21: Couple making love, © The British Museum, London.

Page 24: Couples bathing and making love, © The British Museum, London.

Page 26: Krishna and Radha, © Victoria & Albert Museum, London.

Page 29: Muhammad Shah making love, © British Library, London.

Page 30: Couple making love, © The British Museum, London.

Page 34: Couple making love, © The British Museum, London.

Page 39: Couple making love in a sitting position, © The British Museum, London.

Page 40: Couple making love standing, © The British Museum, London.

Page 43: Couple making love, © The British Museum, London.

Page 44: Couple making love on a sofa, © The British Museum, London.

Page 48: Couple making love, © The British Museum, London.

Page 51: Couple making love sitting, © The British Museum, London.

Page 54: A prince and a lady practicing a Kama Sutra position, painting from the Rajput school, 1790, © The Bridgeman Art Library, London.

Page 57: Couple making love, © The British Museum, London.

Page 58: Couple making love, © The British Museum, London.

Page 61: Couple making love, © The British Museum, London.

Page 62: Girl and prince making love in a Mughal palace, India, late 18th century, Victor Lownes Collection, The Bridgeman Art Library, London.

Page 65: Couple making love on a swing, © The British Museum, London.

Page 66: A man and a woman practicing cunnilingus and fellatio, from an Indian album painting, late 18th century, private collection, Werner Forman Archive, London.

Page 68: "The crow," or "69" as we Westerners know this position. Here a prince and his lady practice cunnilingus and fellatio among cushions on a carpet, Rajastan, Rajput School, 1790, private collection, The Bridgeman Art Archive, London.

Page 70: Couple making love standing, © The British Museum, London.

Page 72: A prince in multiple intercourse, Rajastan, Rajput School, 1800, private collection, The Bridgeman Art Archive, London.

Page 75: Man making love to two women, © Victoria & Albert Museum, London.

Page 76: Couple making love, © The British Museum, London.

Page 79: Couple making love, © The British Museum, London.

Page 80: Couple making love, © The British Museum, London.

Page 83: Couple making love, © The British Museum, London.

Page 86: Woman combing her hair, © Victoria & Albert Museum, London.

Page 88: Couple making love, © The British Museum, London.

Page 90: Couple making love, © The British Museum, London.

Page 92: Couple making love, © The British Museum, London.

About the Author

Manuela Dunn Mascetti was brought up in both Spain and Switzerland. After private education in Switzerland she studied Cultural Anthropology in London at SOAS (School of Oriental and African Studies), part of London University. After her degree she set up the very successful packaging company Labyrinth Publishing with her husband, which was responsible for some of the best-selling and most beautiful books in the late 1980s.

She has written a number of successful books, including *The Song of Eve* (Simon & Schuster, 1990, translated into six languages), *Chronicles of the Vampire* (Viking Studio Books and Bloomsbury, 1991), *Saints* (Ballantine, 1992), the series entitled *The Small Wisdom Library* for Chronicle Books, and many others. Her most recent work includes *A Box of Zen* (Hyperion, 1997), *The Buddha Box* (Chronicle Books, 1999) and *Rumi: The Path of Love* (Element, 1999). Her full list of titles with reviews can be viewed on amazon.com.

She is co-owner of The Book Laboratory Inc, a company that offers consulting on worldwide packaging and publishing and packages books for U.S. and U.K. publishers.